Presented To

_____

By

_____

Date

_____

This book is dedicated to all those
seeking healing, forgiveness,
freedom, and intimacy
with our Lord and Savior.

...In His Presence

*Spiritual poetry
to nurture you
on the path
to holiness*

Kathleen Schubitz

...In His Presence
Intimate moments with your Savior
by Kathleen Schubitz

Published by:
RPJ & COMPANY, INC.
www.rpjandco.com

ISBN-13: 978-0-9819980-1-5
ISBN-10: 0-9819980-1-1

Library of Congress Control Number: 2009913322

Cover Image:
© Olga Khoroshunova - Fotolia.com

Interior Images:
Kathleen Schubitz, © Olga Khoroshunova - Fotolia.com,
© Andrew Kazmierski - Fotolia.com, © fotoliaguy - Fotolia.com,
© fbc24 - Fotolia.com

Consulting Editors: Margaret J. Everett, Melva Bradley

All Scripture quotations used from the King James Version of the Bible.
Used by permission. All rights reserved.

Cover & Interior Design:
Kathleen Schubitz
RPJ & COMPANY, INC.
P.O. Box 160243 | Altamonte Springs, FL 32716 | 407.551.0734
www.rpjandco.com

Printed in the United States of America

Table of Contents

Published by:

RPJ & COMPANY, INC.
www.rpjandco.com

Preface

...In His Presence was birthed through experiences of the Father's love, despite life's tragedies and wrong choices. With a desire to please God in every thought, word, and deed, poetry and prose have been written during quiet times alone with the Lord. As we allow Him to purify us through trials, He sends His ministering spirit, bringing words of encouragement, hope, comfort and transformation.

To receive God's best through this book, read it carefully and prayerfully, a little at a time, or perhaps with repetition, always searching for the hidden nuggets of truth and freedom for your own life. He who knows you and loves you without condition, understands you perfectly, will speak to your heart through the pages of this book, shutting out the world and bringing you into fellowship and intimacy with Himself.

Some poetry will challenge your thoughts, while others will inspire you to greater devotion with the Lord. *...In His Presence* will bless your heart as you open your soul to its living messages and reflect on the scriptures.

This book is a timeless treasure and with it go many prayers that God will enrich every life it touches. So, wherever you choose to be, and whatever you choose to do, let it be done *...In His Presence!*

Kathy

Acknowledgments

Thank you to EVERYONE who has encouraged and inspired me to continue writing poetry.

A special thanks goes to each of my pastors and leaders, past and present. The sermons, words of love and support have given me the confidence to continue writing poetry and allow God to use my expressions of writing to be a blessing to many others.

To my friends, clients and associates for believing in me and providing honest feedback of my writing and my work as a publisher... thank you!

A special thank you to my editorial friend, Margaret Everett. Your knowledge, expertise and giftedness take my written work to a greater level... thank you!

My greatest thankfulness, which words cannot express, is to my Creator and Heavenly Father. Without Him, I would not be here today.

God bless each and every one!

ADORATION

NO GREATER LOVE

I choose to love You
I choose to obey
I choose to serve You
And to walk in Your way.

I choose to love You
I am worthy to be loved
There is none like You
For there's no greater love.

To be happy in this place
Where I find mercy and grace
Longing to be in this place
Dwelling in Your loving embrace.

Greater love hath no man than this, that a man lay down his life for his friends.

- John 15:13

In Your Grace

Forever in Your grace, Lord
I'm forever in Your grace
You cover me, You guide me, Lord
When I seek Your face.

I will find that heavenly place
When I seek Your face.
Bring me to the place, Lord,
Where I rest in Your loving embrace.

For I long to behold you
I long to see Your face,
I love to adore You
As I'm forever in Your grace.

*For the LORD God is a sun and shield: the LORD will give grace
and glory: no good thing will he withhold from them
that walk uprightly.*

- Psalm 84:11

ADORATION

YOU ARE MY EVERYTHING

Come and reign in me
You meet my every need
You are my everything
Lord, come reign in me.

Come in Your holy power
I need You this hour
You are my everything
Lord, come reign in me.

I'll give You all the glory
And all the praise
You are my everything
Lord, come reign in me.

The LORD reigneth, he is clothed with majesty; the LORD is clothed with strength, wherewith he hath girded himself: the world also is stablished, that it cannot be moved.

- Psalm 93:1

GARDEN OF BEAUTY

You're a beautiful rose
Made by God in Heaven,
Colored in purity
In a garden of many.

The tall trees keep you shaded
But the sunlight beams through.
All who choose to sit and enjoy
Will see the beauty He has placed in you.

Jesus extends his right hand
To reach out and admire you,
To capture the moment of
Never-ending beauty inside you.

You are so precious to Him
A hundred others for Him to admire;
His eyes are only upon you
For it is you He desires.

He sees your hidden beauty,
He knows the unfolding taking place.
He can't wait to see you blossom
Full bloom is what He patiently awaits!

*And the LORD shall guide thee continually, and satisfy thy soul in
drought, and make fat thy bones: and thou shalt be like a watered
garden, and like a spring of water, whose waters fail not.*
- Isaiah 58:11

ADORATION

15

A Peek into Heaven

Once upon a ladder
in a vision ever-clear
Up into the clouds it went
just so I could peer.

It was me upon the ladder;
I had climbed all the way up
Little did I know that what I would see
would cause upset.

Resuscitation was needed
but no one was found
My heart ached for my friend
whom I saw bound.

"What can I do, Lord?
How can I help my friend be restored?"

"What shall I do to help her
 live and not die?
Showing me her soul,
what is the reason why?"

"I want to teach you,
dear one
To share truth and love;
help others find freedom."

But the salvation of the righteous is of the LORD: he is their
strength in the time of trouble.

- Psalm 37:39

A WEED...
Willing, Enduring, Everlasting, and Diligent!

Did you ever wonder about the life of a weed?
How do we treat them?
We poison them to make them go away forever.
Greatly determined, we mow them down,
Or we yank them up, hoping they'll never return.

Weeds come in many forms,
Average in appearance, blending with the grass.
Others stand very tall, very noticeable.
Many are so beautiful, that we're sure they're flowers.

Let's be weeds for God;
Stubborn and refusing to die,
We'll always return and live forever.

So, persevere in your walk with God;
Be a weed in the world.
Be strong and persistent with a
"Nothing can stop or kill me" attitude.

No matter what people will do or say
To stop you from being who God called you to be,
Remember the weed, it refuses to be destroyed;
It lives forever and will not die!

I shall not die, but live, and declare the works of the LORD.
- Psalm 118:17

**C
O
U
R
A
G
E**

17

D E L I V E R A N C E

I Matter

Cleanse me, Oh Father
From every sin put upon me.
You've come to heal,
To cleanse and make free.

Long ago men violated my rights
They made me impure.
As I became older
I was convinced to take the lure.

Always harassed and tormented,
I thought it was natural.
To say "No" didn't mean "No"
It really didn't matter.

Jesus came to validate me when I was a pre-teen.
Father longs for the day
When I say "No",
If only because, I matter!

And the very God of peace sanctify you wholly; and I pray God your whole spirit and soul and body be preserved blameless unto the coming of our Lord Jesus Christ.
- 1 Thessalonians 5:23

No More Candy Man

Who is this candy man
that no longer lives?
I used to call him Dad,
but now my Dad is dead.

His candy wasn't worth all the bondage,
torment, and anguish
The temptation of candy
is no longer a desire or a wish.

This man was exposed
and now he must die
Everything that he assured me was truth,
were probably lies.

The candy man is dead
and Jesus is alive.
Jesus brings truth
to destroy every lie!

God is my refuge
and my strength
"Praise God,
the candy man is dead!"

*From the wicked that oppress me, from my deadly enemies, who
compass me about.*

- Psalm 17:9

DELIVERANCE

19

D
E
L
I
V
E
R
A
N
C
E

THE MASTER'S PIECE

There sits an old rocking chair
Outside and tarnished with no one to care.
It doesn't have a home or anyone
To make use of the old rocking chair.

Let's give it a try –
Will it hold me?
Will it be comfortable?
Can I give it a special place?

So I hauled it home like a flirt
Surely it needed love to get rid of the dirt.
I'll bet it's a beautiful piece of wood
Under all the tarnish, paint, and soot.

Too large to dip and clean like silver
It will take time to find the hidden beauty.
So I'll spend time removing and cleaning.
I'll see if what was thrown out for trash
Is now a priceless piece, not tradable for cash.

Sure enough! The old tarnished,
Dirty and thrown away chair—
Is a treasure—cleansed, sparkling and new,
Ready for the Master's use.

You may feel like this old rocking chair
Where life, people or circumstances made you
Feel tarnished and unclean, and life "unfair."
Your Heavenly Father wants to clean you up,
Beautify, and make you His Masterpiece!

No Longer Unforgiven

Being a young child
Forgiveness was a faraway friend.
When I was hurt,
Natural it was to be curt.

Getting up in age
No longer did I want to feel rage.
Though I continued to walk in disobedience
Jesus was filling me with His radiance.

One day I decided to say, "Yes;"
I wanted all the hurt to be erased.
So I painfully agreed to take His hand;
He walked me into the promise land.

He changed my heart!
We're no longer apart.
Gone are the roots of that stubborn tree
Because this life….it's not about me.

Make a choice to let Him,
Then you'll be...No longer Unforgiven.

For if ye forgive men their trespasses, your heavenly Father
will also forgive you:
- Matthew 6:14

LOVE TO FORGIVE

Your love washes over me,
Your love is healing me.
Love comes to wash my sins away,
Forgiveness is closer than it used to be.

Peace draws closer here
Your love removes all fear
You've come, oh Lord, to set me free
Forgiveness with love and peace overtake me.

The Joy of the Lord rises up in me,
Truth and love surround me;
Your joy dispels my enemy,
Love, peace and joy wash over me.

Your love brings truth,
Joy deep in my soul
Your love's exposed the enemy,
Forgiveness with love and truth make me whole.

*And ye shall know the truth, and the truth shall
make you free.*

- John 8:32

PURE LOVE

Sexual impurity
is gone from me.
It has no more power
It's cut off for life.

It tries to harass me
But I know I am free!
Thank you, You're greater,
Greater than he.

God sees me as pure
Washed in Jesus' blood
Now I'm brand new
Walking in pure love.

*But if we walk in the light, as he is in the light, we have fellowship
one with another, and the blood of Jesus Christ
his Son cleanseth us from all sin.*

- 1 John 1:7

F
R
E
E
D
O
M

23

A Reason to Shout

Plucked out
Turned about
Should I shout?
I wanted to pout!

Lived in a house
Quiet as a church mouse
He acted like a louse
Then discovered mad cows.

Alone and afraid, I faked the praise
Something in me needed to be raised
Above my circumstances and the mess
Above everything, mostly myself.

Can't see a way out of the chaos
Seems like forever I'd be homeless and moneyless
So deep in debt, and full of despair
No one, anywhere, even seems to care.

God's Word says he loves me
Unworthy is how I felt inside of "me"
How could He ever love me?
I didn't feel worthy of being loved and free.

F
R
E
E
D
O
M

So many churches from which to choose
Choosing the right door, I knew I couldn't lose
Warmed the seats every chance I had
Eventually, the enemy would get tired and mad.

But You've planted my feet upon the Rock
For Your name's sake, I know I'll be mocked
You've called me to dwell in the promise land
To live in a house not built on sand.

Determined to be free from the enemy's hold
Now I no longer fit the "mold"
Your hand and Your heart, You gave to me
Now I know, You'll never forsake me.

Redeemed and restored
You're forever my Lord
You've turned my life inside out
Now I have a reason to shout!

Mine eyes are ever toward the Lord;
for he shall pluck my feet out of the net.
- Psalm 25:15

FREEDOM

DECLARATION OF FREEDOM

I declare I can hear
I declare I can see.
I declare I can learn
I declare I can speak.

I declare I have clarity
For in You I have victory.
I declare I have no more disease
You died for my every infirmity.

I declare no more weakness
For in You I have meekness.
I declare I am healed
For with Your blood I am sealed.

I declare and believe
Your Word over me.
I declare, forever
Forever I am FREE!

But now being made free from sin, and become servants to God, ye
have your fruit unto holiness, and the end everlasting life.
- Romans 6:22

26

COME AWAY WITH ME

Lay down your burdens,
Open up your heart;

Lay down your burdens,
Let the healing start;

Lay down your burdens,
And be set free;

Lay down your burdens,
Come away with Me!

HEALING

O come, let us worship and bow down: let us kneel before the LORD our maker.

- Psalm 95:6

27

LOVE OF FAITH

A young girl named Faith
So innocent and pure;
God has made you so beautiful
You are so precious for sure.

God has never left you,
He has always protected you;
He washes away the memories,
His love will bring truth.

Cleanse her,
O Father
From every sin
Put upon her.

Washed and cleansed
He removed all the hate.
Come take His hand,
And walk with love and faith.

Sing and rejoice, O daughter of Zion: for, lo, I come, and I will dwell in the midst of thee, saith the LORD.

- Zechariah 2:10

THANK YOU

Thank you, Lord Jesus,
I thank You today.
I thank You for healing
And for coming my way.

Thank You for the gifts
You put within each of us.
Thank You for using
And blessing all of us.

Thank You for loving
And making us free.
Thank You for dying
And setting captives free.

*But we are bound to give thanks alway to God for you, brethren
beloved of the Lord, because God hath from the beginning
chosen you to salvation through sanctification of the
Spirit and belief of the truth:*
- 2 Thessalonians 2:13

HEALING

FATHER'S TOUCH

Touch the hearts of Your people
Renew them once again.
Let their hearts not be feeble
But restore and strengthen them.

Touch the hearts of Your people, Lord
Bring Your fire to purify.
Make the hearts rejoice only in You
Then the sons shall multiply.

Touch the hearts of Your people
Remove their hurt and pain.
Replace the stony hearts in people
With a heart of flesh, to gain.

Touch the hearts of Your chosen
To bring Your heart to the nations.
For those that cannot be frozen
You fill and refill, with Your holy radiation.

*Flee also youthful lusts: but follow righteousness, faith, charity,
peace, with them that call on the Lord out of a pure heart.*
- 2 Timothy 2:22

CELEBRATING LIFE

Eight, new beginnings,
With Him my life is worth living.

Eight years ago,
A story once told.

Life, as I knew it was nearing the end
Time for tormenting seemed to be without end.

Life had been spared
All alone in despair.

Where do I go?
Who can I tell?

Who can I trust?
No one will believe that I did what I must.

Alone in the dark
Afraid of the threat

Jesus appeared to be distant
Prompted to cry in an instant.

The meaning of life became new
Searching my heart through and through.

Now testifying to God's love without strife
Living and celebrating eight years of new life!

*But God commandeth his love toward us, in that, while we were
yet sinners, Christ died for us.*

- Romans 5:8

HONORING YOU!

Lord, I want to honor You.
Teach me to give honor in all I say and do.

Help me to stand firm in my conviction.
So when I stand before You, there is no friction.

When I stand firm, I can say
God honors me and expects others to obey.

Oh, Father in Heaven, help me to stand
As I choose to grab hold and take Your hand.

I will stand my ground
And will not frown.

When others don't understand
I've chosen You to be my man.

*If any man serve me, let him follow me; and where I am, there shall
also my servant be: if any man serve me, him will my Father honour.*
                                                    - John 12:26

TREE OF LIFE

A tree of life
is a righteous soul,
No matter your size,
God has made you whole.

Be a tree full of leaves,
vibrant in color,
Your trunk size may be different—
it really doesn't matter.

Be a tree full of life,
willing to share wherever you stand,
Stand righteous, bearing good fruit,
willing to give a hand.

A tree of life
thrives on living water,
Sunshine and shade
it is never without.

Righteous trees,
eternal and full of life;
trees of life we are,
made righteous, and without strife.

*And he shall be like a tree planted by the rivers of water, that
bringeth forth his fruit in his season; his leaf also shall not wither;
and whatsoever he doeth shall prosper.*

- Psalm 1:3

JUST DREAMIN'

It's a beautiful sunny day,
Me and Jesus are walking in a field.

He chooses beautiful flowers
To make me a bouquet.

Such love, such joy, He has
Just spending time with me.

Skipping and laughing,
We begin to run, and fall down.

No hurts, no sense of failure
For He is there to lift me up.

Me and Jesus, just dreamin'.

Unto thee lift I up mine eyes, O thou that dwellest in the heavens.
- Psalm 123:1

BE

I've not called you to do,
But I've called you into being.
When you are being you're not doing;
And when you're being I can be…Me.

When you're doing, they don't see Me;
When you're being I can rest.
When you're being you'll worship Me;
And when you're being, people will be blessed.

I've not called you into doing
For doing only makes you weary.
I've called you into being,
So when I speak or work through you
It can be Me, and I get the glory.

Being gives you my identity
It makes you equal with Me.
Your doing makes you work;
Your being represents Me.

So make a decision today,
To BE and not DO
For in your being…
People will see Me!

*Being justified freely by his grace through the redemption
that is in Christ Jesus:*

- Romans 3:24

HEAVEN OR HELL?

Heaven or Hell —
Which one do you choose?
The one you surrender to
Knows the other will lose.

Heaven or Hell —
It's not a game, not a chance, but a choice.
Games in life can be serious and cause harm
The choice is easy—no multiple choice.

Heaven or Hell —
Do you think it's a place?
It's a choice you make this day
Your life's mistakes supernaturally erased!

Heaven or Hell—
A place in the mind
It's all how you think and how you see
That determines what your life will be.

Heaven or Hell — Which will you choose?
Life or death; love or hate,
Health or sickness; freedom or bondage,
Peace or turmoil; blessing or curse?

Heaven or Hell —
What will it be for friends and family?
What will it be for the wrong-doers
that you call your enemy?
Whatever you choose will be the choice
you make—for you, for your destiny!

- Inspiration from a Mark Rutland Message

ALWAYS, I AM

Will you dance with Me?
I am always before thee
Standing in position ready,
For My beloved to dance with Me.

Will you dance with Me?
Will you take My hand?
Will you allow Me to cover you?
I will help you to stand!

How I do love thee!
I'm always before and around thee.
My hands upholding and embracing,
I remain, ready and waiting!

His left hand is under my head, and his right hand doth
embrace me.

- Song of Solomon 2:6

COME

My hearing's improved
I heard the Lord say
"Come take My hand
You'll not go astray.

"Come sit here with Me
And rest at the well
Refreshing and refilling
I make all things brand new.

"Come talk to Me
Come walk with Me
Come take My hand
I'll show you the way."

*Sing and rejoice, O daughter of Zion: for, lo, I come, and
I will dwell in the midst of thee, saith the LORD.*
- Zechariah 2:10

Take My Heart

Take my hand
so I will walk with thee.
Hand in hand,
You and I will be.

I long to be
heart to heart;
Nothing will ever
pull us apart.

You are the breath
that makes me sing.
You are the wind
beneath my wings.

Take my hand
and walk with me
To a place I'll be
forever with thee.

And ye now therefore have sorrow: but I will see you again, and your heart shall rejoice, and your joy no man taketh from you.
- John 16:22

GOD'S CONTRACT

What does it say?
Will He want to do business with me?
Will He meet me half way?

Will He compromise the quality to
what He has in store?
Will He devalue my product,
and pay less rather than more?

The answer, my friend is in you.
The answer, for Him,
is His word of truth.

He will not overcharge,
He will not trade you in;
His promise to pay for your life
is forever, it will not end.

Your value is a price set up high
His word, He will honor
regardless of price.

How about you?
Will you honor your word?
Will you give Him what He's already paid for?

He paid for your weakness,
He paid for your sin
Doubtful He'll turn His back on you,
the Bible says He lives within.

Will you share all your hurts
and give Him your heart?
He'll help you always,
He'll never depart.

With His blood,
the contract's been signed
Consider His love for you,
will you sign on the dotted line?

All He asks is that you love
and obey His command
To love one another,
forgive and be free in this land.

God's contract was signed,
sealed and delivered.
It will not lose value;
it will never expire.

The terms have been set;
the blood has been shed.
The price for you has been paid,
so give Him your best!

*And I will make an everlasting covenant with them, that I will not
turn away from them, to do them good; but I will put my fear in
their hearts, that they shall not depart from me.*
- Jeremiah 32:40

CALL TO THE QUEEN

I've crowned you My queen;
Why do you not see
What others do to you
When I hear your heart scream?

You are My daughter,
You are My queen;
Please keep yourself only for Me.

Guard your heart,
Protect your surroundings,
For your heart calls to the King.

I love you and I adore you,
You are forever in Me—
And I call you My Queen!

And the king loved Esther above all the women, and she obtained grace and favour in his sight more than all the virgins; so that he set the royal crown upon her head, and made her queen instead of Vashti.
- Esther 2:17

NEVER LOST

My child, how I love thee,
My child I hold you so dear.
My child you are so precious,
And you are so near.

Do you know how special you are?
Do you know how much I care?
Do you know that where you are
Is better for you there?

How beautifully God has made you!
How wonderful it must be,
That you are in His presence
And I must wait to see.

- Love, Mom

*For the Son of man is come to seek and to save
that which was lost.*

- Luke 19:10

I'LL ALWAYS REMEMBER...

I'll always Remember,
How beautiful God made you.

I'll always Remember,
Every birthday, every holiday,
you never forgot to send a card;
And every trip you were on,
you sent a favorite postcard.

I'll always Remember,
How you loved cats and how they
brought you so much joy.

I'll always Remember,
You loved and gave so freely
to everyone you met.

I'll always Remember,
How you loved to labor and give at
Christmas time.

I'll always Remember,
when you lived in Florida—
how you unselfishly labored to
pick and juice oranges and grapefruit—and then
gave the fruit of your labor away.

I'll always Remember,
The walks we took together
and the strolls on the beaches.

I'll always Remember,
The day you told me,
"You know, I would die for you."

I'll always Remember,
You were just like Jesus!

- In loving memory of a sister

A good name is better than precious ointment; and the day of death
than the day of one's birth.
- Ecclesiastes 7:1

Heart Comfort

Words cannot express
You are so blessed!

You now must know
God is with you even when you're low.

He's always had a plan,
Now He'll bring you to the promise land.

Reach out to others and you will see
God knows and provides for your every need.

Put Him first, talk to Him,
He wants you to give Him your thick and thin.

In your weakness He is strong
He's closer now than you thought long.

Day after day
The sorrows will fade.

Your loved one is gone, but not far
The Father in Heaven makes them close in heart.

Blessed are they that mourn: for they shall be comforted.
- Matthew 5:4

SEED OF LOVE

You've stirred in me
A gift you see
A gift of giving
I'm sure to receive.

The gift is Jesus
The name above all names
His name is Jesus
The greatest gift from God.

You've stirred in me
You've planted a seed
A seed of love
One that can't be unseen.

The gift is Jesus
The name above all names
His name is Jesus
The greatest gift of all.

You've stirred in me, a gift you see
You've planted a seed, and now I believe
Love from God will grow and grow
Inspired by your seed of love.

And the LORD thy God will circumcise thine heart, and the heart
of thy seed, to love the LORD thy God with all thine heart,
and with all thy soul, that thou mayest live.

- Deuteronomy 30:6

47

Be it Unto Me

I am called Your righteousness
I am loved and free
I am crowned with precious jewels
By God who lives in me.

Because I'm filled with Father's love
I can walk in faith, and live in peace.
My heart radiates with light from above
Strife, hatred, and vengeance must cease.

When I take Your hand, Lord
You will always lead me.
When I take Your hand, Lord
You will forever guide me.

According to thy word
I'm filled with love and glee.
When I take Your hand, Lord
Your love envelops me.

Your word
Your love
Your truth
Be it Unto me!

...Behold the handmaid of the Lord; be it unto me according to thy word.

- Luke 1:38

THE VOICE OF LOVE

**L
O
V
E**

The voice of love
draweth me
The voice of love
speaks to me
The voice of love
instructs me.

The voice of love
draws me near
The voice of love
is so dear
The voice of love
makes my way clear.

The voice of Father's love
flows from beginning to end
The voice of love
in His presence will not end.

*My sheep hear my voice, and I know them,
and they follow me:*
- John 10:27

DADDY'S GIRL

Because He first loved me
I can smile whatever life may bring.
I am free to dance as He leads me
He loves when I use my voice for singing.

Because He first loved me
I can lend a helping hand.
You and I can pray together
He made us friends in this land.

Because He first loved me
I can walk and not crawl;
He teaches me to write and speak
Because of His love, I can stand tall.

Because He first loved me
I know His love is real,
He made me to be me
That's why I know, I'm Daddy's girl!

O come, let us worship and bow down: let us kneel before the LORD our maker.

- Psalm 95:6

LIVE IN LOVE

The depth of wisdom from God above
How could it be without His love?

Love He has for me and you
Tested and tried, forever true.

No matter the choice
You can hear His voice.

He's calling His people, this is true
He'll make all things once old, brand new.

Will you trade in your old wineskin?
He promises to remove all your sin.

Will you heed His voice of love?
Will you walk with wisdom from above?

He'll give you His best
He has the answers to pass every test.

Walk with wisdom, live in love
His banner over you — He made it Love!

*To him the porter openeth; and the sheep hear his voice: and he
calleth his own sheep by name, and leadeth them out.*
- John 10:3

OBEDIENCE

NO OTHER WAY

Your ways lead me to You
Always refreshing and new,
Your way is righteous
And it brings me to You.

I choose to obey, Lord,
To walk in Your way,
I choose to speak words
of kindness and pray.

Jesus, You are my life
And You are my love,
You are my everything
Sent from Heaven above.

There's no one like You
You've made me brand new.
You've done everything
So I choose to trust You.

There's nothing undone
And nothing to repay;
You've done everything
So I choose to obey.

But this thing commanded I them, saying, Obey my voice, and I will be your God, and ye shall be my people: and walk ye in all the ways that I have commanded you, that it may be well unto you.
- Jeremiah 7:23

MY SON

OBEDIENCE

I've called you Son,
Don't be a child.
A Son can feast
But the child whines.

A Son can relax
A child, he can't sit still;
A Son will hear instruction,
A child pays no mind.

Be a child no more,
Let the son stand up;
Sit that child down,
Let My son come forth.

*And because ye are sons, God hath sent forth the Spirit of his
Son into your hearts, crying, Abba, Father.*
- Galatians 4:6

53

O B E D I E N C E

MESSAGE IN THE STORM

The storm is raging;
Can you hear what it says?
Is God calling you to sit and be still?
Is He calling you to trust in Him?

He is a jealous God,
Do you know He is your source of life?
He is your breath and strength,
Without Him you would not exist.

God says, don't fear—
For perfect love casteth out fear
His love covers a multitude of sin,
For His love and peace dwell within.

His call is for you—
Will you take heed, listen and obey?
He's calling and waiting for you
To respond to His call and not be afraid.

His love lights the way through the storm.
His love toward you is Father's best.
His love will not cast you aside;
Everything—love, peace, and joy,
within you, resides.

- Written During Hurricane Charley
August 13, 2004

Know ye not, that to whom ye yield yourselves servants to obey, his
servants ye are to whom ye obey; whether of sin unto death,
or of obedience unto righteousness?

- Romans 6:16

BEAUTIFUL DAY

It's a beautiful day
and the Lord wants to say,
Come take My hand,
come Walk with Me.

I'll lead you and guide you,
So come follow Me.
I'll lead you and guide you,
I'll teach you all things.

For today is the day
that I will rest in your love,
Today is the day that
I call you My Love.

I love you, my child,
I love you with pride,
Forever I'll love you,
I'll be by your side.

I'll never forsake you,
Always I'm with you,
I'll always pursue you,
and I'll always be with you.

- Love, Jesus

*The Lord thy God in the midst of thee is mighty; he will save, he
will rejoice over thee with joy; he will rest in his love,
he will joy over thee with singing.*

- Zephaniah 3:17

REST

In Your presence, Lord,
Here I find rest.
Nothing to ruffle a feather,
Not even the weather.

Clouds may come to bring rain
It can't stop me from giving You praise.
Sunshine permeates life's haze
Even when I feel a bit crazed.

Here I am, Lord,
Desiring Your rest.
Come here to me, Lord,
I'll give You my best.

You've come to make new,
Refill, and refresh.
Come where You are, Lord,
Bring me Your rest.

Come unto me, all ye that labour and are heavy laden,
and I will give you rest.

- Matthew 11:28

JESUS

Jesus, the soft and gentle breeze
Brushes along my back
While the breeze blows
through my hair;
I hear the sound of birds talking.

Jesus, the gentle whisper
As the butterfly flies overhead,
The birds keep singing,
Flies buzzing around my head.

Jesus, the gentle nudge
It's so quiet out here,
yet I hear Him speak;
Thoughts of beautiful friends
With whom I wish our time would never cease.

Jesus, the call to me
To sit and talk with Him,
To listen and write,
To give Him praise, for
with Him everything's all right.

*Jesus said unto him, Thou shalt love the Lord thy God with all thy
heart, and with all thy soul, and with all thy mind.*
- Matthew 22:37

WHO AM I?

Lord, because of who You are
You tell me to believe.
I am worthy, I am cleansed;
I am lovely, I am free.

I am loved and I am blessed
I'm your beloved and You want my very best.
You seek to find me, to tell me
I am called Your righteous tree.

I am Your eyes and your ears
As your sheep, Your voice I'll hear.
I am Your hands and Your feet
You tell me there's no defeat.

For in You I am strong
Forever I'll sing Your song.
I am healed and I am sealed
Your shed blood made the deal.

I am bought and I'm paid for,
You say, my sins are no more.
On the cross You paid the price for me,
You say, the I AM now lives in me.

Because of who You are
I can rest in You, and know You're never far.
I cannot doubt, but must believe,
that I am, what the Word says I am.

But of him are ye in Christ Jesus, who of God is made unto us
wisdom, and righteousness, and sanctification, and redemption:
                                                 - 1 Corinthians 1:30

THANKSGIVING

A time to be grateful
Put away all things hateful

We can live without strife
He paid the price for our life

Circumstances can alter our attitude
Attitude will determine our altitude

We can enjoy every day we're living
Because the Lord keeps on giving

Wondering and guessing
How He keeps on Blessing

Remember your loved ones
You're a cared-about someone

With thanksgiving in our heart
We can each do our part

With thanks and with giving
We've got something with which to praise Him!

*And whatsoever ye do in word or deed, do all in the name of the
Lord Jesus, giving thanks to God and the Father by him.*
- Colossians 3:17

PUTTING ON THE ARMOR

I put Jesus on my mind,

Jesus guides my feet,

Jesus is the word

That lives inside of me.

Jesus all around

And living within';

Jesus, Jesus

I love Him!

Put on the whole armour of God, that ye may be able to stand against the wiles of the devil.

- Ephesians 6:11

COME TO ME

Come Holy Spirit
Come Lord, I pray;

Send Your anointing
Please send it today.

Come down in power
I need You this hour;

Come Holy Spirit
Come Lord, I pray.

Behold, the hour cometh, yea, is now come, that ye shall be scattered,
every man to his own, and shall leave me alone:
and yet I am not alone, because the Father is with me.
                                        - John 16:32

WALKING IN VICTORY!

Today I choose
To declare and decree
God's words of truth and love
Will forbid the enemy.

Words contrary to life will not come out of my mouth
Your fight for me makes me strong and stout
Guard my tongue, life's biggest vice
So I'll no longer be accused of strife.

You will overpower the enemy's attack in my head
It's by Your spirit that I am led
I will no longer give in and feel defeat
While You take your place in the driver's seat.

I declare and decree this hour
I will give the enemy no power
I will give the enemy no place
It is you, O Lord, that keeps me in grace.

PRAYER

I will not curse,
I will no longer criticize
I will speak words of love and life
Because in me, You reside.

Today I declare and decree
To forgive all who served the enemy
Today, I declare and decree
I'm freely walking in victory!

*For whatsoever is born of God overcometh the world: and this is the
victory that overcometh the world, even our faith.*

- 1 John 5:4

63

MORE OF JESUS

When I look for love
I see more of Jesus
When I see Jesus
I want to be more like Him!

With more of Jesus in my life
I'll live in love, not in strife
Lord, I've made a mess
More of Jesus, I must confess.

Come flood my soul
Lord, make me whole
Fill all my pores
I need Jesus, more!

But we see Jesus, who was made a little lower than the angels for the suffering of death, crowned with glory and honour; that he by the grace of God should taste death for every man.

- Hebrews 2:9

PROMISES FOR A NEW YEAR

P
R
O
M
I
S
E

A new day in a new year
We can give God praise or live in fear

Are we expecting
Or rather accepting

Of past choices we've made
Or declare all things become new this day?

Do we embrace our past and speak a wish
Or will we unashamedly proclaim our list?

Hearts need to be fixed on Heaven above
To declare and expect of His boundless love

Let's give God praise for His mighty reign
Always leading and pursuing us through life's maze

Clarity and direction will eventually come
Testifying with praise of victories won!

Proclaiming Your greatness in this New Year
Promises galore if we'll obey and not fear!

*Having therefore these promises, dearly beloved, let us cleanse
ourselves from all filthiness of the flesh and spirit,
perfecting holiness in the fear of God.*
- 2 Corinthians 7:1

WAKE UP!

Wake up, Wake up!
It's time to stand up.

Wake up, hear the call,
Jesus is your all and all.

Wake up, no need to fear,
If you'll listen, you will hear.

The voice of God is calling…
Wake up! Are you listening?

He's calling you to higher ground,
Will you take heed and not frown?

He says there's a purpose for your life,
A life of love, and not of strife.

Love your neighbor, love yourself,
Lend a hand; learn to look beyond yourself.

Wake up, don't look back,
With God there is no lack.

PROMISE

Wake up, take a stand,
Be bold and take His hand.

You're His eyes and ears, hands and feet.
When you follow Him, there's no defeat.

Wake Up! He'll lead you to the promise land!
Wake Up!

*The Lord is not slack concerning his promise, as some men count
slackness; but is longsuffering to us-ward, not willing that any
should perish, but that all should come to repentance.*

- 2 Peter 3:9

P
R
O
V
I
S
I
O
N

BLESSING TO BLESS

Bring in the money
Bring in the dough;
Let it come running
Make it overflow.

Always You are paid first
You meet my every need;
I know I'll never thirst
Your fountain waters every seed.

I'll never beg for bread
And I'm never without shelter.
You're the blood that was shed
You're the drink that's a satisfier.

Bring in the money, Lord,
So we can help those in need.
Bless everyone, Oh Lord,
So we can bless one another.

Bring ye all the tithes into the storehouse, that there may be meat in
mine house, and prove me now herewith, saith the LORD of hosts,
if I will not open you the windows of heaven, and pour you out a
blessing, that there shall not be room enough to receive it.
- Malachi 3:10

His Way

We shall lend and not borrow
Let's not wait until tomorrow.

Every day that we're living
We can keep on giving.

The choice is up to us
Will we, in God's word, trust?

When we give with gratefulness
He'll send His love and faithfulness.

Giving out of love today
His provision for us will always make a way.

*The LORD shall open unto thee his good treasure, the heaven to
give the rain unto thy land in his season, and to bless all the
work of thine hand: and thou shalt lend unto many nations,
and thou shalt not borrow.*

- Deuteronomy 28:12

PROVISION

P R O V I S I O N

YOU ARE...

The answer to every question
The provision for every need.

The tower so high
Shelter as the storm draws nigh.

Holy and righteous
My glory and grace.

My strength and my shield
To Your Holy Spirit, I yield.

You are holy, mighty, loving
Full of favor, mercy and grace.

A mighty fortress in my life
You are... Everything!

But the God of all grace, who hath called us unto his eternal glory
by Christ Jesus, after that ye have suffered a while,
make you perfect, stablish, strengthen, settle you.

- 1 Peter 5:10

HAPPY BIRTHDAY...

A birthday is a special time to say,
Thank you to my mom,
Thank you to my sister
And thank you for being my friend!

Happy birthday
With blessing and upon blessing
And year after year,
May the Lord keep blessing you!

If I told you, "Happy Birthday, Jesus,"
I would not be telling a lie.
I tell you, "Happy Birthday, Jesus"
Cause He's in you and I.

Thank you, Jesus,
For making such a special friend;
Thank you for bringing us together,
And for a treasure without end!

Happy Birthday to my special friend!!!

A man that hath friends must shew himself friendly:
and there is a friend that sticketh closer than a brother.
- Proverbs 18:24

SPECIAL PRAYER

A Prayer of Blessing

Bless her, Lord Jesus,
Bless her I pray
You'll lead her and guide her
Clearly show her the way.

Speak to her spirit
Clear her overwhelmed mind
A pure heart to hear You
A beautiful spirit to receive.

She loves and adores You
She honors and obeys
She's always in Your presence
You always make a way.

I know You'll never leave her
You'll always protect her
I know that You're with her
Lord, bring her to the place of peace, today.

The Lord bless thee, and keep thee: The Lord make his face shine
upon thee, and be gracious unto thee: The Lord lift up
his countenance upon thee, and give thee peace.
- Numbers 6:24-26

A Daughter's Prayer

Bless my mother, Lord, I pray
Touch her heart; lead her in your way.

Bless her for all her giving
Prosper her in living.

For all the hurt and pain I've caused,
Let the moment come to pause.

I want to erase the mistakes I made
There she'll see the price You paid.

She always thought I was hard to understand;
Lord, let her know I unknowingly took Your hand.

Mom, you truly are a blessing to me!
May the Love of God shower down upon thee!

- Written from the Heart

But when it pleased God, who separated me from my
mother's womb, and called me by his grace,
- Galatians 1:15

DINNER WITH THE KING

May I come to Your table, Lord?
Will You make me a place?
May I join You in this feast?
O Lord, that you call me to partake?

Prepare me for Your table, Lord,
Make me pleasing to You;
Prepare me for Your feast, Lord,
In all I say and do.

Prepare the garment!
Prepare the song!
Prepare my heart!
To be with you long.

The table is set
For the King and I.
"Come to the table," says the Lord,
"I long to adore my beautiful bride."

Then the king made a great feast unto all his princes and his servants, even Esther's feast; and he made a release to the provinces, and gave gifts, according to the state of the king.
- Esther 2:18

MY JESUS

Jesus, my Jesus
My Lord and my love;
Send down Your spirit
Descend like a dove.

Jesus, my Jesus
My savior and love;
Send down Your spirit
And fill us with love.

Jesus, my Jesus
My God and my King,
Send down Your gladness
And make our hearts sing.

And he hath on his vesture and on his thigh a name written,
KING OF KINGS, AND LORD OF LORDS.
- Revelation 19:16

ANOINTED LOVE

Jesus, anoint these fingers,
Anoint my heart and soul.
Jesus, anoint Yourself in me,
You've come to make me whole.

Jesus, anoint me where You are;
Your eye's always on me, I know You're never far.
Jesus, Your anointed love,
Come and touch my longing heart.

Jesus, with Your amazing love
Come and touch me now.
Jesus, Your anointed love
Is greater than anyone's.

Jesus, Your anointed love
Is deeper than the deepest sea.
Jesus, Your anointed love
Brings me back to thee!

For I know the thoughts that I think toward you, saith the LORD, thoughts of peace, and not of evil, to give you an expected end. Then shall ye call upon me, and ye shall go and pray unto me, and I will hearken unto you. And ye shall seek me, and find me, when ye shall search for me with all your heart.   - Jeremiah 29:11-13

QUIET WILL

Lord, help me be quiet
Help me be still.

I need to hear Your voice
I want to do Your will.

Help me be quiet
Help me be still.

Teach me to think on the words You say
Teach me to be led all of my days.

Teach me to be still and sit here with You;
For I long to dwell in your presence,
The presence of Your perfect will.

*That ye would walk worthy of God, who hath called you
unto his kingdom and glory.*
- 1 Thessalonians 2:12

WORSHIP

INDEX with Scripture References

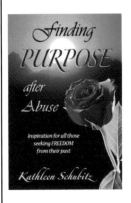

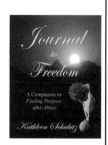

Published works by RPJ & Company

Destined for Healing
by Marty Delmon

Destined for Success
by Marty Delmon

Finding Purpose after Abuse
Inspiration for all those seeking freedom from their past
by Kathleen Schubitz

If the Battle is the Lord's... Why Am I So Tired?
by Randy Newberry

Journal to Freedom
A companion to Finding Purpose after Abuse
by Kathleen Schubitz

Scripture Keys for Finding Purpose after Abuse
Inspiring words for your journey
by Kathleen Schubitz

Writing Your Life Story with God as Your Guide
by The Rev. Aileen Pallister Walther, Deacon

You Are Loved
by Patricia A. Elston

Waterscapes Calendars - 2010 & 2011
by Margaret J. Everett

Check our these and more books at:
Any online bookstore, Amazon.com and
www.store.rpjandco.com.

About the Publisher

In 2004, the Spirit of God birthed RPJ & Company according to Romans 14:17.

RPJ & Company, Inc. began publishing Christian books for pastors, leaders, ministers, missionaries, and others with messages to help the Body of Christ. Our published books continue to empower, inspire and motivate people to aspire to a higher level of understanding through the written word.

Our company is dedicated to assisting those individuals who desire to publish Christian books that are uplifting, inspiring and self-help in nature. We will be expanding our line to include Christian children's books. We also offer assistance for those who would like to self-publish.

The special service that we provide is customized, quality layout and design for every client. This gives every new author a chance at becoming successfully-published. For every book, we offer exposure and a worldwide presence to help the book and the author become discovered!

"As an author and publisher, I can guide you through the steps of creating, editing, proofreading and provide you with a professional layout and design for any printed item, one you'll be proud to call your own."

- Kathleen Schubitz
Founder and CEO

RPJ & COMPANY, INC.
"Where quality and excellence meet face to face!"

www.store.rpjandco.com

Order Form

Email orders: kathy@rpjandco.com
Visit us on the web: www.store.rpjandco.com

Telephone orders: 407-551-0734

Postal orders: RPJ & Company, Inc.
P.O. Box 160243 | Altamonte Springs, FL | 32716-0243

Name: _____

Address: _____

City/State: _____

Zip code/Country: _____

Telephone: _____

Email: _____

Please send _____ copy(s) of book(s) indicated below. Telephone orders will ship out the next business day; other orders are shipped after payment is received.

___ *Finding Purpose after Abuse* $25.95 x _____ = _____

___ *Scripture Keys* (companion) $12.95 x _____ = _____

___ *Journal to Freedom* (companion)
     Print book $28.95 x _____ = _____

     on CD $19.95 x _____ = _____

___ *...In His Presence - B/W* $11.95 x _____ = _____

___ *...In His Presence - COLOR* $17.95 x _____ = _____

Shipping & tax Included
Subtotal _____

Order total enclosed _____
    (money order only)

We accept: VISA / MASTERCARD / DISCOVER
Discounts are available for quantities of 10 copies or more.
Call or write us for details.

* 9 7 8 0 9 8 1 9 9 8 0 1 5 *